JANUARY BRINGS THE SNOW

Sara Coleridge

A Seasonal Hide-and-Seek

Elizabeth Falconer

ORCHARD BOOKS
A division of Franklin Watts, Inc.
New York

Editor's Note: Sara Coleridge, in her verse for August,
has used the word *corn* in the sense in which it was used in Britain at that time,
to refer to what in present-day America
would be called *wheat*.

Illustrations copyright © 1989 by Elizabeth Falconer.
First American edition 1989 published by Orchard Books.

Orchard Books
A division of Franklin Watts, Inc.
387 Park Avenue South
New York, NY 10016

Orchard Books Canada
20 Torbay Road
Markham, Ontario 23P 1G6

Originally published in the United Kingdom by
William Heinemann Ltd., London

Printed in Singapore
by Tien Wah Press (Pte) Ltd

10   9   8   7   6   5   4   3   2   1

Library of Congress Cataloging-in-Publication Data

Coleridge, Sara Coleridge, 1802–1852

   January brings the snow: a seasonal hide-and-seek book: poem/
Sara Coleridge; Elizabeth Falconer. – 1st American ed.
p.   cm.
   Summary: Each month brings something new and different in this
rhyme about the changing seasons. Movable flaps conceal a mouse
family in various seasonal situations.
   ISBN 0–531–05824–7
   1. Months – Juvenile poetry. 2. Seasons – Juvenile poetry.
3. Children's poetry, English. 4. Toy and movable books – Specimens.
[1. Months – Poetry. 2. Seasons – Poetry. 3. Mice – Poetry.
4. English poetry. 5. Toy and movable books.] I. Falconer,
Elizabeth, ill. II. Title
PR4489. C2J36 1989
821′.7 – dc 19   88–28609
                                                                         CIP
                                                                         AC

For Nicola and Toby

January

January brings the snow;
Makes the toes and fingers glow.

February

February brings the rain,
Thaws the frozen ponds again.

March

March brings breezes loud and shrill,
Stirs the dancing daffodil.

April

April brings the primrose sweet,
Scatters daisies at our feet.

May

May brings flocks of pretty lambs,
Skipping by their fleecy dams.

June

June brings tulips, lilies, roses;
Fills the children's hands with posies.

July

Hot July brings cooling showers,
Strawberries and gilly-flowers.

August

August brings the sheaves of corn,
Then the Harvest home is borne.

September

Warm September brings the fruit,
Sportsmen then begin to shoot.

October

Fresh October brings the pheasant;
Then to gather nuts is pleasant.

November

Dull November brings the blast,
Then the leaves are falling fast.

December

Chill December brings the sleet,
Blazing fire and Christmas treat.